AF612642

A SHORT HISTORY OF POWER

Author: Ioannis Pappas
ioannispappas19@gmail.com

Title: A Short History of Power

Text editor: Aikaterini Aristidou
Translator: Despina Avgoustaki
Cover designer: Petros Anastasiou
Cover image: Freepik

ISBN 978-618-00-2711-2

Ioannis Pappas

A SHORT HISTORY OF POWER

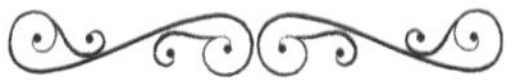

CONTENTS

Prologue

History– along with geography– is something I've been reading about as a hobby since I was young; I think these two go together. I wanted to get a picture of the lands where the events took place. Very little has been written about power, about how the citizens were ruled by their sovereigns –perhaps that's the most important. Wars, battles, strategies, numerical superiority, military innovations, history is full of these, as well as conquests, taxation, looting, violence. About power, though, about how they ruled over the citizens or if they ruled over them at all, nothing. Thus, I decided to write *A Short History of Power* because I believe that if we are able to study the system of power that controls our life, maybe, just maybe we will find some solutions to important problems.

The impetus for writing this was given to me in Germany where I found myself in the past seven years, working long hours in heavy yet well-paid manual labor. Germany is a country that opens its arms and embraces every immigrant.

I borrowed the term "kameradism" from the German language (*kamerad*: comrade) after noticing a picture of the solidarity circle urging team spirit among the employees (a picture of five hands in a circle, one holding the wrist of the other) posted in certain companies. Whenever I'd meet Mr. Kitsos, we would talk about current affairs and he would ask me, "Why is all this happening?" If he could read this book, he'd get an answer.

I should clarify that I use foreign terms for names and places, while I refer to the latter by their current names.

I would like to thank Mr. Charilaos Economou, since it was from our conversations that I gathered basic information on *Kameradism,* which I wouldn't have found otherwise and which filled gaps in my knowledge. I would also like to thank Mr. Efstathios Papazisis and Mr. Nikitas Varitimos for their help in publishing the book.

Ioannis Pappas

Change

I used to visit Germany every summer during the last three years of the 20th century. Two cases remain carved in my memory, not so much because they were different from the ones I was used to but due to the 180-degree turnabout their development took. Germany is a country with an extended road network. About 10% of its territory is roads. Twenty years ago, there were no roundabouts at all, unlike France, where they made the most out of the advantages conferred by roundabouts, placing them at almost every junction. Over the past twenty years, German streets have filled with roundabouts, replacing the crossroads. An equally impressive change happened with the use of sunglasses. In the summer afternoons of 2000, while I was walking around the busy pedestrian streets of Germany, I was the only person wearing sunglasses. They weren't even sold in stores, and why would they be since no one needed them? Twenty years later, sunglasses can now be found on shop shelves while more than half of the citizens use them.

Two 180-degree changes from black to white, from night

to day. But there is a difference: in the first case, the about-turn was a result of an official decision, aiming to raise the living standards of the citizens. In the second case, the change was dictated by the need to protect the eyes by the citizens themselves, due to the climate change.

Whenever the leaders, those in charge, spot their mistakes, they rush to correct them once they realize that, at this point, the advantages outweigh the disadvantages or the conditions are appropriate. Therefore, there is always room for radical changes if new ideas come to light, are examined, approved, and implemented. As long as they do not conflict with the basic principles of power.

Power

"Power: Ability derived from entitlement or the power to impose one's will on others, to control (an individual, group, community, country, etc.)." (G. Babiniotis, *Dictionary of the Modern Greek Language*, 3rd edition, 2008). It is power that pulls the strings, decides who will work, where, and how much. It determines who will be recruited and for how long. Until the beginning of the last century, it was power that determined who would live and who would die in cases of famine.

A large percentage of the population of developed countries is familiar with the system of power that governs our lives (school, socialization, groups, obedience, the consequences of its actions). It's not taught anywhere; it can't be found in books nor can it be taught in classrooms. It's what old people used to call the "school of life". It is introduced in the lives of children from a young age and it is confirmed daily for life. Empirically, older people pass it on to the younger ones. Its principles, what it's based on, what it needs, what it lacks, have never been mentioned. Its rules, where and when it started, how it spread, and which system of power existed before it, have never been written. Through the study of our system of power, solutions to many unsolved problems may be found.

Studying our system of power, we understand why sub-Saharan Africa finds itself in such a tragic situation. Why India, Bangladesh, Pakistan, and many other Asian and Latin American countries have very low per capita income. We realize why one in about 150 citizens of the United States is in prison or why 2.8% of their population is in prison, has a suspended sentence or is on probation. Almost 1 in 35 citizens. By studying our system of power, we can also find out where the decision-making process aiming to protect the environment is stuck.

Human societies have always had their leaders. They were the ones in whose hands the fate of the citizens was placed. It was they who undertook the task of ensuring the citizens' security, housing, food, clothing, and when enough money was left over, their entertainment. They were the ones who created powerful hegemonies, empires, and kingdoms through expansionist wars, offering more security to their citizens.

Oligarchism

In the spring of 334 BC, after securing his kingdom from the neighboring peoples, Alexander the Great campaigned against Persia with an army of 40,000 men. After many battles, sieges, and endless marches, he managed to overthrow the Persian Empire. By force of arms, one charismatic leader replaced another in power. The Macedonians faced the same problems as their predecessors. They relied on an oligarchy of satraps who were forced to send their children hostage to the centers of the empire in order to prove their allegiance. A tactic that would remain until the time of Louis XIV, the Sun King (le Roi Soleil), who built Versailles to house "envoys" from all over France.

Later on, a more powerful army, the Roman one, gradually reached the Macedonian kingdoms and took its turn in power through conquests. The Roman Empire brought a change to the power relations by introducing the Senate. The oligarchs were united and made decisions as a group. The Byzantine Empire, as a continuation of the Roman Empire, also relied on a form of oligarchy.

By the end of the 8th century, we had the creation of the Carolingian Empire, which was based on the feudal system. In this case, the slaves went up a step while the free citizens went down a step. Thus, everyone became a serf. The system of power remained an oligarchic one. The structure of society reached as high as knighthood. The hundred or so families who toiled to equip and support the knight and his entourage were all serfs. They had no say in anything. As in every oligarchic system, the feudal lords/oligarchs didn't trust the serfs, they were afraid of them since they existed only to work. They avoided arming them out of fear of their turning the weapons against them. When you do not arm citizens for fear of their turning against you, then you do not exercise power over them.

We find a hereditary takeover of power in oligarchy, which in turn causes unpredictable situations. The heir is not necessarily the best of the society he is called to rule over. So in an oligarchy, there is a small percentage of citizen control, 1-3%, and an unsatisfactory way of taking power. The principles of oligarchy are:

a) It has a leader (duke, king, emperor).

b) The leader relies on an oligarchy.

c) The oligarchy does not dominate the citizens, but it depends on their cooperation, which stems from their need to live peacefully.

d) The stratification of society reaches the heads of settlements, villages.

e) The assumption of power is inherited at all levels.

Observing the characteristics of the oligarchic power, it is no wonder nor is it accidental that the oligarchic hegemonies collapsed like paper towers with the arrival of the people of the North. It was the system of assuming and maintaining their power with its inexhaustible dynamics that pushed them to create hegemonies to the borders of the then known world. They established hegemonies in Russia-Belarus-Ukraine, in Southern Italy, in Normandy, and in the British Isles. A system of assuming and maintaining power stratified to the base of society. A system that draws its power from the base but also relies on it. A power that integrates 100% of its citizens, transforming them into active members of society.

Kameradism

Norway is a country in Northern Europe whose territories include the northwestern part of the Scandinavian Peninsula. If one wants to go from its southernmost to its northernmost end, one has to travel about 2,000 km by boat. Its coastline, including the fjords, is 22,000 km long, while it reaches the length of 83,000 km when including its 50,000 islands. A characteristic of the fjords is that the sea often flows up to 200 km inland. On the sides of the fjords, there are tall, vertical, rocky masses that give the impression that one is at the bottom of a gorge. The rocks are sparsely set aside, giving way to small arable land that can sustain a small number of families.

The people of Norway lived in a huge, sparsely populated area, usually on remote farms. The sea route was the most appropriate way, if not the only one, to connect them. Under such circumstances, the oligarchy was never developed; it could not prosper. There were no villages with a concentrated population and a specific leader, from which one could collect taxes under the threat of a strong army. Nor could someone do the same to isolated farms, as it would be unprofitable due to the great sea distances.

On the eastern side stood high, unapproachable mountains while on the western side stretched the ocean, two natural barriers that protected the Norwegians. There, in order to protect themselves from each other (man's worst enemy is his own self), they developed a system of power completely different from the one developed in the rest of Europe and Asia: *Kameradism*, which depends on the base of society. The cell of *Kameradism* is the team. Five neighboring farms, five men, one leader. Especially after they figured out how to promote the most capable, intelligent, charismatic person, they put themselves at his disposal for anything, wherever and whenever he needed them. Their relationship, their cohesion was powerful and always remained so wherever they were. The unity of the group was its armor. The sense of security acted as a centrifugal force. United they were significant and strong. Each person had his companions, he was not alone; in times of need, he would have them by his side and when they needed him, he would be there for them. A team where everyone's word counted and decisions on issues that concerned them were made collectively.

In the same way, five team leaders from the wider region were united in a group, the leader of which emerged following the same process. The most capable, intelligent, charismatic became leader. Their society was stratified in exactly the same way to the very top, where five people were always placed. Decisions regarding issues of their respective stratum and below were made as a group. A perfect system of power without gaps. Were one to disappear at any point in the hierarchy, one could be immediately replaced; there was no power vacuum. It relied on its base, so its power extended to 100% of its citizens. It utilized the abilities of the citizens to the greatest degree possible, elevating the capable ones, placing them where they should be. It did not fear its citizens turning against it, since it was made up of them. Soon, this system spread through Scandinavia and from there to the rest of the world.

It encountered many difficulties in its course. It had to face the status quo, the different customs and traditions, the political events, the habits, and the financial situations of the areas it attempted to settle. Although the Viking raids had already begun by the end of the 8th century, there is one incident I consider to be undeniable proof that the people of the North acted in an organized way, with a plan, a common administration, and the aim of controlling all of the then known world.

San Paolo di Civitate is a lowland village in southern Italy, located 40 km north of Foggia. There, on the morning of June 17, 1053, two troops confronted each other. On the one side stood the Normans who had just conquered Apulia, and on other stood Pope Leo IX, who had assembled an army consisting of Swabians and Lombards –the German emperor Henry III had refused him any help, as had the French king. The Byzantine emperor Constantine IX, though solicited, did not send help either. The battle that followed was fierce and continued until half of the Pope's Army was slaughtered and the other half retreated in disarray. The Normans respectfully surrounded the pope and escorted him to the monastery of Benevento where he remained confined for the last 9 months of his life, negotiating with the victors. It was this pope, who, during the period of his confinement, authorized the legates he sent to Constantinople to cause the schism with the Eastern Church. In this way, he set the boundaries between the Western and the Eastern Church. The Byzantines of the schism became the enemies of the pope and the Normans became the guarantors of his security. From that point onwards, the pope stopped asking the Byzantines for help while for the next 400 years it was they who asked and begged for his help. In August 1059 in Melfi, Pope Nicholas II bestowed upon the Norman Robert Guiscard the title of Count of Apulia, Calabria, and Sicilia. The Normans had not yet set foot in Sicily and the pope had no rights over the island. Most importantly, however, the pope stripped the two emperors of their claim to Southern Italy.

If anyone wanted to go from Western Europe to the Byzantine Empire safely, the key was Southern Italy. From there, a person could safely travel to Greece, Constantinople, or the Holy Lands. That's why the Byzantines insisted so much on maintaining and expanding their conquests in the area. After the battle of San Paolo di Civitate, it was clear that the Normans were operating according to a plan. While they had not even completed the conquest of Southern Italy nor had they set foot in Sicily, they used the Schism to express their interest in the Byzantine Empire. A handful of Normans managed to consolidate their power in Southern Italy within twenty years. A power that relied on the foundation of society and drew strength from the entirety of its citizens. The first part of the conquest of one-third of Sicily's territories was achieved with 150 knights and an infantry of 500:

"Only from the slaughter and chaos of the fifteenth century could such a family have emerged triumphant, and only by continuing the slaughter could they secure their position." (Dan Jones, *The Wars of the Roses: The Fall of the Plantagenets and the Rise of the Tudors*, 2014).

Of course, the chaos that Dan Jones is talking about refers to the transitions in leadership and the shifting alliances. England's economic structure functioned normally. True chaos would have ensued if this system of power had not existed. It is precisely this description by Jones that fits the way power was assumed and maintained in *Kameradism*. However, it is not only a phenomenon of the fifteenth century but a permanent element that began in the Viking Age and continues to this day, merely in a milder form following the Second World War. Technology, the mass and social media bring about the same results in a more peaceful way, so to speak.

In a nutshell, *Kameradism* has the following eight principles:

a) Society must be evenly stratified from top to bottom in groups.

b) Each group should consist of 3-5 people and have a leader.

c) Even at the top level, there should be a group of 3-5 people.

d) Make sure to elevate the people with the highest IQ (the smartest, most capable). The higher we go up the social pyramid, the smarter the people we meet should be, with the ones with the highest IQs at the very top.

e) Its members should trust, respect, and consciously obey the leadership. They should feel a sense of belonging.

f) No person should be left out; everyone should belong somewhere.

g) Humility.

h) The higher, the safer (a continuous effort to ascend).

Only through the daily grind do capable and smart citizens emerge. This book cannot help anyone climb the ladder of power. This can be done only through the internal processes and requirements of society. After all, the main things citizens have to keep their focus on are the two basic values of the education they have received: humility and obedience.

These are the principles of *Kameradism* that drove it forward and allowed it to spread. Not everywhere though; there is one exception where it cannot be developed. For it to be able to penetrate a human society, this society must have an average IQ score of at least 90. Otherwise, *Kameradism* cannot work, it loses its coherence, its control. This explains why countries in Asia, Africa, Central and South America have failed to grow economically. One would expect India to have a rate of development similar to that of China, considering that as a colony of England for hundreds of years under capitalism, it should have reached the levels of China decades earlier or, at least, be in a position to compete with it. But it happens to be the only exception of *Kameradism*, without which you cannot rely on the majority, on the basis of society, and you cannot have the production you decide on. According to the narratives of classical English writers, the citizens of England worked under dire conditions for hundreds of years to build and elevate their state to what it is now. At this point, I want to clarify that this approach is not racist. A nation of people with an IQ below 90 are certainly capable of working and contributing as well as everyone else. This is evident from those who emigrate to developed countries. They work and perform at their job; they are a small minority that is absorbed by the system of power. It is one thing to "take an active part in power" and another to "offer to work hard".

Borders - Navy - Trade

If one reads the history of the 11th century and onwards, as well as the daily news, which is nothing more than daily history, we can see and understand the episodes/events we experience every day. Whatever occurs at the top or any other part of the social pyramid also happens in all of its levels. If there is an episode/event at the top, the same episode/event will be replicated at the base. Numbers should not scare us; people come together in the exact same manner, whatever their level might be.

It has been mentioned that the 11th century is the golden age of the Normans due to their brilliant achievements. Normans was the name the French used to refer to the people of the North, the Vikings. The Vikings ended their invasions of France around 911-920 AD, when the Frankish king Charles III recognized their rule in Normandy in exchange for France's protection from their countrymen's invasions. Their leader, Rollo, became a vassal of the king and acquired the title of the Duke of Normandy. The Vikings shared a common religion and language, manners and customs, as well as a common system of power, *Kameradism*. They were a sea people, the routes of their communication, trade and food passed through the sea. It is no surprise that they were excellent seafarers. Once they made some progress with the hull of their ships, the sail, and the rudder, they began to make their existence known to the rest of Europe. They rowed, fought, colonized, transformed themselves into farmers, traded up to thousands of kilometers away from their homeland, and were recruited as mercenaries. The vast majority, however, remained in their homeland and lived a rural life. It is estimated that 10th century Denmark had a population of 700,000. By analogy, we can estimate that along with Norway and Sweden, they must have reached 1.2-1.5 million inhabitants. They could have easily expanded, and they did. They were most probably informed about what they would encounter at their target areas by their trading network. They were familiar with and took advantage of the discord prevalent in the Frankish kingdoms and in England, which was divided into seven kingdoms, as well as the fragmented power in Ireland. They faced no difficulties in Russia, Belarus, and Ukraine, as there was no strong opposition.

Borders were fluid at the time. They weren't stable. Fiefdoms changed lords often, what with the arranged marriages, the dowries, the inheritances and the conquests. The people of the North realized the importance of stable borders as a fundamental administrative principle and set the first fixed border in history, one that would last for more than a thousand years. In 808 AD, King Gudfred of Denmark built

Dannevirke, a fortification along the neck of Jutland, Denmark's only land border, limiting the spread of the Franks. A border that remained intact until 1871, when the Germans moved it 40 kilometers further north with the unification of Germany and the establishment of the German state. In the late 11th century, the Normans established their kingdom in southern Italy, demarcating their only land border, on the northern side, which had been in place for over 800 years, until it was abolished with the unification of Italy and the establishment of the Italian state in 1861. The British Isles had no need for borders as there was a sea wall separating them from mainland Europe. That was the greatest advantage the people of the North spotted and proceeded to conquer them. They were a strong naval force, if not the only one. If they managed to maintain their naval superiority, they could spread *Kameradism*, safeguarding it from their strong base. They achieved all three.

One of the most important advantages of the Vikings was their dominance over the sea and the waterways. It seems that no one tried to compete with them or no one could. They monopolized the waterways outside the Mediterranean, so it is safe to assume that they must have monopolized the maritime trade as well. At this point, we should add that land trade was expensive and precarious, so we understand the significance of trading by sea and rivers, especially for long distances. Trade offered many benefits to those who conducted it. The motivation, the driving force, was profit. Merchants used to come in contact with other traders in distant or close hegemonies. They were familiar with their manners, customs, strengths and weaknesses. They would get in touch with the respective merchants, exchange information, and cooperate with them in the cities they visited. They would certainly serve as ambassadors or consuls, if we can call them that, and could act as intermediaries between their own ruler and the rulers of the area in which they traded.

In June of 860 AD, 200 Viking ships manned by 8,000 men set out from their hegemony centered in Kiev, crossed the Dardanelles, and appeared under the walls of Constantinople in the Sea of Marmara. Emperor Michael III and the navy were absent on a campaign against the Arabs. The Vikings, after looting the outskirts of the city and the Princes' Islands, returned to Kiev. The emperor sent a delegation to the Rus region to investigate the matter. They eventually reached a written trade agreement concerning the Viking's commercial actions in Constantinople and their privileges. This was just the beginning as in the next century similar fleets would threaten Constantinople four more times. Each invasion was followed by negotiations and agreements with the dominant element being the trade of the people of the North in Constantinople, the increase of their privileges, and their admission to the imperial army as mercenaries. Towards the end of the 11th century, the baton had passed to the Venetians and other Italian cities.

In the East

In 753 AD, the Vikings established their first base in Russia at the lake of Staraya Ladoga, east of Saint Petersburg. From there, via rivers and the portage of their ships they reached the rivers Volga and Dnieper. The Volga led to the Caspian Sea, to the Islamic world, while the Dnieper to the Black Sea through Kiev and from there to Constantinople. The journey to Constantinople was a dangerous and arduous one. Even in our days it seems extreme. The Vikings, though, kept making this trip, carrying goods and troops for three hundred years. They would pass the Baltic Sea through lakes and rivers; there were several river roads in the Dnieper. In order to leave behind the rivers that flow into the Baltic and reach the Dnieper that flows into the Black Sea, they would have to tow the ships and carry the goods for several kilometers. From there, they had to sail another 1,200 km to the Black Sea. There were 11 points where navigation was not possible due to waterfalls and rushing waters. So, in order to bypass these points, they would take the ships and the cargo out of the water, over and over again, and carry them up to the point where it was possible for them to continue sailing. They were probably the only ones who used these routes that even today sound unreal. In Russia-Belarus-Ukraine, the people of the North established a hegemony whose first center was Novgorod and then Kiev. There, in the East, they became known as the Rus or the Varangians. In 987 AD, at the request of the emperor Basil II, Vladimir of Kiev sent 6,000 Varangian warriors that helped Basil suppress the revolts of two powerful landowners. In return, Basil gave his sister Anna as a wife to Vladimir, who agreed to be baptized and to Christianize his people. It is from this hegemony in combination with the Orthodox Christian faith that the Russian state later emerged. Henceforth, the Varangians would constitute the personal guard of the emperors, while at the end of the 11th century they'd be replaced by the English. They would contribute significantly to the expansion and the consolidation of the empire during the reign of Emperor Basil II, the Bulgar Slayer.

In the South

The Normans arrived in southern Italy in 1017 as mercenaries, having been Christianized many generations earlier. In 1930, the Duke of Naples ceded the County of Aversa as a fiefdom to the Norman Rainulf. In 1059, the Normans ruled almost all of southern Italy. It was then that the pope appointed the Norman Robert Guiscard as Count of Puglia, Calabria, and Sicilia, retaining sovereignty over these areas, displacing the claims of eastern and western emperors. The Normans, having extended their power to the base, to the people and drawing strength from them, campaigned in 1081 AD and defeated the Byzantine army of Emperor Alexios Komnenos in Albania and Greece. They had to rush back, though, to confront Emperor Henry IV of Germany who had taken advantage of their absence. Henry, who was in Rome, did not even fight and upon hearing the arrival of a large powerful army, gathered his forces and returned to Germany.

The hegemony of the Normans, after conquering Sicily in 1091, would play a crucial role in the Crusades, as well as the development of the crusader states. At the end of the 12th century, the kingdom of the Normans would pass under the rule of the German emperor in a curious way that as Michael Psellos states, "We ordinary mortals are unable to understand." While Richard I of England was returning from the Third Crusade, he was afraid to travel through France and, for unknown reasons, did not want to cross the Straits of Gibraltar either. So he arrived in Croatia (according to one version, he was shipwrecked in Corfu), he disembarked and secretly attempted to cross central Europe. Somewhere in Austria, he was recognized, captured and handed over to the German emperor Henry VI. The emperor demanded the great sum of 150,000 marks as ransom for his release. As soon as he received it, he encamped in southern Italy, which he conquered by defeating the Normans in battle. In 1266, again by force of arms, the kingdom would pass to the French, while in 1282, after the Sicilian Vespers, the first successful revolution in history would cause the kingdom to pass to Spain (Aragon) at the request of the Sicilian rebels.

In the West

By early August 1066, the Duke of Normandy, William, had amassed an army of about 8,000 men and the ships to carry them off the coast of Normandy. He would invade England, claiming his right to the throne, having made sure to receive the pope's blessings. At the same time, another man, Harald Sigurdsson, king of Norway, had gathered an equivalent army with the necessary ships to take it to England, also claiming his right to the throne. There was intelligence shared between the two sides and each man knew the other's movements. A few weeks later, the Norwegian king made the first move, crossed into England and, on September 25, confronted the British army and its king, Harold Godwinson, at Stamford Bridge.

The battle that followed was fierce and bloody. Only a few Norwegians managed to get back on their ships and set sail. On September 28, after William received the news of the Battle of Stamford Bridge, he sailed to the opposite shore at Hastings. As soon as Harold was informed, he rushed straight to the south to face the threat. On October 14, the two armies met in Hastings. At nine in the morning, the battle that would change the fate of England as well as the whole world was launched. Soon after King Harold fell dead, his soldiers disbanded. William was the victor of the battle and, on December 25, he was crowned King of England in London. It would be another 20 years before he imposed his rule on the whole country.

The greatest change brought about by William the Conqueror was the fiefs he gave to his 5,000 followers. According to the Domesday Book, there were 300,000 families in England, meaning that one person in every sixty families was his follower. Automatically, his influence spread throughout the country through them. His followers had nothing more to do other than what they had learned: they spread *Kameradism*.

They gave the people power, they were not their tyrants; they were the ones the people trusted and followed, as they in turn did their king. They adopted the Viking soul that rowed, fought, cultivated, colonized at their leaders' request, because they, too, were with them and obeying their own leaders. The barons were not afraid of the citizens because both parties knew that their course and interests were common. Decisions relevant to them were made as a group at every level, and the most perceptive individuals emerged as leaders. What more could a person who is a member of society want?

In the period of 1277-1282, Edward I campaigned in Wales. The Welsh used the longbow. A typical longbow was 180 cm long. The English copied it and prevailed on the battlefields for the next 300 years. The longbow was described as the atomic bomb of the time –it had a range of 320 meters, a speed of 12 shots per minute, the ability to pierce through the armor, and was used by the common people. The crossbow had the same range and piercing ability, but only one shot per minute, and was used by mercenaries. The main force of the European armies was the knights, who, faced with the longbow, had no time to approach, let alone get involved in battle, neutralized as they were by the shots of the English archers. In a pitched battle against archers with longbows, if the soil was dry and the horse could develop a speed of 40 km per hour, it took 30 seconds for the blockaded cavalry to reach the archers from the moment it entered their range, allowing them six shots. In the best-case scenario, the knight's horse would be injured and he would be taken as a prisoner, released in exchange for ransom. This explains the disproportionately high number of French victims and prisoners of the British during the Hundred Years' War.

When Edward encountered this weapon, realizing its value, he banned all sports in England and made it mandatory for all men capable of carrying a bow to practice archery in their spare time. To stay alert, an archer had to practice daily. The longbow required a lot of strength to bend –studies done on skeletons have shown that archers suffered from a curvature of their spine caused by the strain required to bend the bow. Daily training was a painful process that left permanent health problems.

The barons had trust in their people, they did not fear

them. They equipped them and used them for the emergence of the British Empire. More important than the archers was the commitment of the citizens to their rulers. The king ordered them to take up arms and they did, without taking the cost into account. He knew that wherever he sent them, they would be loyal to him, they would never betray him, and that's what he did; he sent them all over the world to conquer it, which they did. In the meantime, the oligarchic rulers were afraid of their citizenry; it was their most dangerous enemy. How could it not be when they did not have full control over them? This explains why for more than 300 years no hegemony ever managed to replicate the longbow, and had to concede to English supremacy.

The people of the North were familiar with the advantages of the British Isles. After all, their own lands had the same benefits. Norway and Sweden were protected by a sea wall. In order to attack them, one needed a strong navy. Half of Denmark was made up of islands while the other half, the neck of the peninsula, was unsafe for an aspiring invader, as he would be in danger of being sidelined by a naval force. In detail, the advantages of the British Isles are the following:

a) They have a central position in Europe, a high number of citizens, and cover a large area, so they can develop a strong hegemony.

b) They are not easily invaded. They have no need for a permanent army. Permanent armies are expensive. The constant problem of hegemonies was the army. Its recruitment, payment, equipment, logistics and everything else related.

c) The creation of a merchant marine. The islands need supplies, but they export products too. If they back their own merchant ships, they will dominate the sea by equipping the merchant ships and converting them into warships in case of war.

d) Easy cultivation of diversity, a key feature of later nation-states. The units of measurement, their way of driving, all prove how easily the British cultivated diversity compared to mainland Europe.

e) Absolute control over the movement of citizens-goods. Nobody and nothing leaves or enters without permission.

Summing up the short history of the people of the North and at the same time the history of their power's expansion, *Kameradism*, we should not forget that along with their spread to the eastern tip of Europe, they did not fail to spread to the westernmost parts of the world that they discovered, Iceland and Greenland. They colonized these lands, building the first defensive wall there as well; they did not know what was beyond that point, and they never needed to.

Vikings

For the first time in history, a people appears that will for 300 years continuously send military forces and settlers, thus embracing the entire known world. One thing is for certain, they did not intend to build a great empire. Their system of power did not need an empire, it was against central control. This became clear in 1053, after the battle of San Paolo di Civitate, when the pope asked the Normans to leave Italy and return to their homeland before the battle.

What is perhaps the most important point to focus on is that he blamed the Normans for what the Vikings were usually accused of –looting, theft, unprovoked violence, catastrophic rage– at a time when more than half of the soldiers standing on the opposite side against him were civilians from the areas the Normans had supposedly committed all these atrocities. An accusation completely contrary to the Normans boastful declarations that they bring security and abolish crime in their lands, in accordance with the legend circulating in Normandy about the three gold rings. The violence they exercised was nothing more than an act of assuming and maintaining their power that relied on the base. In essence, they took the citizens out of obscurity and gave them the floor; if they deserved it, of course. With his opposition, the Pope showed that either he had no idea what was going on or that he had suicidal tendencies. After the battle of Civitate, the people of the North sent the message that their system of power was superior and that they operated in groups, with principles and a central plan.

Yes, the Vikings blended in wherever they went: assimilation was not against their principles, their soul though was bequeathed to us; it lives through us, it lives with us.

Without a solution?

In the United States of 2013, there were 2,150,000 prisoners and 4,750,000 adults had a suspended sentence or were on probation. 40% of the prisoners were African Americans, about 860,000 individuals. The total number of African Americans in the country was 40,000,000. 20,000,000 of them were men and if we subtract the minors, 20%, we find that 1 out of 18 adult males are in prison, or 1 out of 6 are either in prison or have a suspended sentence or are on probation. The numbers alone are tragic. In Alabama, one in three African Americans will go to jail once in their lifetime. Are African Americans criminal by nature? The answer is no. In Europe, the corresponding numbers are lower than those of the whites. So what's going on? The suggestion that it is a policy of certain companies to make money from their free labor is not valid. The USA is a rich and prosperous country. It is implausible that some people pass laws to put citizens in prison and then make money from their free labor.

The answer lies in the restriction of *Kameradism*. A glimpse into the IQ of sub-Saharan Africa will disappoint us. Citizens with low IQ can definitely work, they can clearly offer just as much as their colleagues–they can live normally, have families, cook, have hobbies, and, in any case, do what all normal people do. The one thing they cannot do is adapt to our society. They are maladapted for the society of *Kameradism*. It is impossible to integrate into society by reading books. Integration into society goes through what is not visible to humans. And that is because a person is not what we see, but what we cannot see, his mind, his IQ - that's what he will rely on in order to work with his fellow human beings in groups. Thus, the segregation and isolation of African Americans were not abolished in 1970, they just changed name.

There seems to be no solution; if there were, it would have been found. A large number of maladapted people in a state is like a bomb at its foundations. If there were a solution, it would have been found - is there anyone who does not want all citizens to be active members of society? Perhaps if a research team is formed, made up of citizens with knowledge and experience, lawyers, economists, educators, high-ranking security officials, humanitarian organizations, based on the principles and rules of *Kameradism*, they will eventually come to conclusions and decisions that if implemented, will manage to integrate their fellow human beings into society.

When it comes to Hispanics, the numbers are better. They constitute 16% of the US population and 20% of the prisoners. One out of forty-four adult males is in prison and one in sixteen is in prison or has a suspended sentence or is on probation. The average IQ of Hispanic America is 80-85.

Immigrants are essential in developed societies. New immigrant hands must constantly be admitted. Without them, society will begin to decline. An entry ban would be destructive, if not impossible. Solutions can be found for the immigrant issue if it is studied and decisions are made. The system has no racist momentum. Whatever one's race, sexual orientation, age, religion, culture, everyone is accepted, as long as they are able to integrate into society. Europe does not face the same immigration problems as the United States; it draws immigrants from Eastern Europe. Those coming from Asian or African countries are an easily absorbed minority. The Chinese, a people with a high IQ, do not face such problems; they meet their needs with their domestic immigration.

Epilogue

From the moment the system of power that governs our lives, *Kameradism*, began to spread beyond the region where it was born, the world started to change. The more it spread, the more the world changed. All the goods and services we enjoy today, such as food, housing, clothing, health, longevity, education, and entertainment are its creations. It highlights the capable ones, relies on the base, has control, is not afraid of discoveries, innovations, ideas, science. Instead, it brings them to the surface, tests them and, if it is in the interest of society, adopts them. After 1053, the oligarchic system of power kept losing ground despite its resistance. It was afraid of everything new –ideas, science, education– it was afraid of losing its power to smarter, more capable people. Oligarchy would still have us in the fields, sowing wheat with beasts and reins, as they did in some parts of southeast Europe even in the beginning of the 21st century. Of course, along with the benefits came the destruction of the environment and climate change. Our planet has now set its limits. It remains to be seen if we will be able to respect them.

About the author

Ioannis Pappas was born in Greece (Nea Vyssa, Evros) where he graduated from high school. He worked for twenty years as a freelancer. For the past eight years, he has been working as a driver for a transport company in Germany.

Bibliography

Amato, Raffaele, *The Varangian Guard 988 – 1453*, Osprey Publishing, 2014.

Angold, Michael, *Η βυζαντινή Αυτοκρατορία από το 1025 έως το 1204 μία Πολιτιστική Ιστορία*, μτφ. Καργιανιώτη Ευαγγελία, εκδόσεις Παπαδήμα, 2008.

Anderson, Perry, *Το Απολυταρχικό Κράτος*, μτφ. Αστερίου Ελένη, εκδόσεις Οδυσσέας, 2003.

Anderson Perry, *Από την αρχαιότητα στον Φεουδαρχισμό*, μτφ. Αστερίου Ελένη, εκδόσεις Οδυσσέας, 2001.

Αντρέεφ, Ιγκόρ – Λεσένκο, Λεονίντ, *Δοκίμια Ρώσικης Ιστορίας*, μτφ. Νικολάου Ναταλία – Καλογερόπουλος Πέτρος, εκδόσεις Εν πλω, 2015.

Asimov, Isaac, *Το χρονικό των Επιστημονικών Ανακαλύψεων*, μτφ. Μπαρουξής Γιώργος – Σταματάκης Νικηφόρος, Πανεπιστημιακές εκδόσεις Κρήτης, 2008.

Asimov, Isaac, *Το Χρονικό του Κόσμου*, μτφ. Σταματάκης Νικηφόρος, Πανεπιστημιακές Εκδόσεις Κρήτης, 2006.

Bartlett, W. B., *Vikings a History of the Northmen*, Amberley Publishing, 2019.

Berstein, Serge – Milza, Pierre, *Ιστορία της Ευρώπης από τη Ρωμαϊκή Αυτοκρατορία στα Ευρωπαϊκά κράτη 5ος – 18ος αιώνας*, μτφ. Δημητρακόπουλος Αναστάσιος, εκδόσεις Αλεξάνδρεια, 1997.

Blöndal, Sigfús, *The Varangians of Byzantium*, translated, revised and rewritten by Benedikt S. Benedikz, Cambridge University Press, 2007.

Brawnworth, Lars, *The Sea Wolves: a History of the Vikings*, Crux Publishing, 2014.

Breuers, Dieter, *Εις το Όνομα Τριών Δαιμόνων, το Κυνήγι των Μαγισσών στον Μεσαίωνα*, μτφ. Γεωργούλα Ευαγγελία, εκδόσεις Κονιδάρη, 2008.

Bushkovitch, Paul, *Ιστορία της Ρωσίας*, μτφ. Σπανού Θάλεια, εκδόσεις Αιώρα, 2016.

Cannon, John – Griffiths, Ralph, *The Oxford Illustrated History of the British Monarchy*, Oxford University Press, 1988.

Dorling, Kindersleybook, *Firearms an Illustrated History*, Dorling Kindersleybook, 2014.

Duby, Georges, *Παγκόσμιος Ιστορικός Άτλας*, μτφ. Λεβαντοπούλου Μαρία – Ράπτης Χαράλαμπος – Φλιτούρης Λάμπρος, εκδόσεις Πατάκη, 2001.

Δαμηλάκου, Μαρία, *Ιστορία της Λατινικής Αμερικής*, εκδόσεις Αιώρα, 2015.

Ferguson, Nial, *Η Εξέλιξη του Χρήματος - μία Οικονομική Ιστορία του Κόσμου*, μτφ. Παγουλάτου Ευτυχία, εκδόσεις Αλεξάνδρεια, 2011.

Freedman, Paul, *Μπαχαρικά και Μεσαιωνική Φαντασία*, μτφ. Σιδέρη Ντίνα, εκδόσεις Κονιδάρη, 2010.

Freeman, Melville, *The Story of Our Republic or The Romance of America*, F. A. Davis company publishers, 1942.

Fuller, J.F.C., *Η Ιδιοφυής Στρατηγική του Μεγάλου Αλεξάνδρου*, μτφ. Κολιόπουλος Κ., εκδόσεις Ποιότητα, 2004.

Grant, R.G., *Μάχες: Η Πολεμική Ιστορία 5.000 χρόνων*, μτφ. Λαμπρινάκης Δημοσθένης, εκδόσεις Anubis, 2008.

Grimal, Pierre, *Η Ρωμαϊκή Αυτοκρατορία 27 π.Χ. – 476 μ.Χ.*, μτφ. Χοροσκέλης Δημήτρης, εκδόσεις Θύραθεν, 2004.

Harvey, Alan, *Οικονομική Ανάπτυξη στο Βυζάντιο 900 – 1200*, μτφ. Σταμπόγλη Ελένη, Μορφωτικό Ίδρυμα Εθνικής Τραπέζης, 1997.

Haves, James, *Μικρή Ιστορία της Γερμανίας*, μτφ. Παππάς Ανδρέας, εκδόσεις Πατάκη, 2018.

Hindley, Geoffrey, *Οι Σταυροφορίες: Μία Ιστορία για τους Ιερούς Πολέμους των Σταυροφόρων*, μτφ. Κατσέλης Δημήτρης, εκδόσεις Ενάλιος, 2007.

Jones, Dan, *The Wars of the Roses. The Fall of the Plantagenets and the Rise of the Tudors*, Penguin Books, 2015.

Konstam, Angus, *Ιστορικός Άτλας της Μεσαιωνικής Ευρώπης*, μτφ. Αυγουστίνου Παρασκευή, εκδόσεις Σαββάλας, 2005.

Konstam, Angus, *Ιστορικός Άτλας των Σταυροφοριών*, μτφ. Γεδεών Δημήτρης, εκδόσεις Σαββάλας, 2006.

Kean, Michael Roger, *Ιστορικός Άτλας της Βυζαντινής Αυτοκρατορίας*, μτφ. Κατσικερός Αθανάσιος, εκδόσεις Σαββάλας, 2006.

Κωτούλας, Ιωάννης, *Βίκινγκς οι Αδάμαστοι Πολεμιστές του Βορρά*, εκδόσεις Περισκόπιο, 2006.

Loades, Mike, *The Longbow*, Osprey Publishing, 2013.

Lock, Peter, *Οι Φράγκοι στο Αιγαίο 1204 – 1500*, μτφ. Κουσουνέλος Γιώργος, εκδόσεις Ενάλιος, 1998.

Logan, F. Donald, *Οι Βίκινγκς*, μτφ. Αστερίου Ελένη, εκδόσεις Οδυσσέας, 2007.

Μαγουλάς, Δ. Αντώνιος, *Η Ιστορία των Ηνωμένων Πολιτειών της Αμερικής. Οι Ρίζες του Αμερικάνικου Ονείρου 1600 – 1990*, εκδόσεις Ακίδα, 1997.

Maalouf, Amin, *Οι Σταυροφορίες από τη Σκοπιά των Αράβων*, μτφ. Βάντση Αγγελική, εκδοτικός οργανισμός Λιβάνη, 1983.

Maurois, André, *Ιστορία των Ηνωμένων Πολιτειών 1492*

– *1946*, μτφ. Φλώρος Παύλος, εκδόσεις Κουλτούρα, 2015.

Maurois, André, *Ιστορία της Αγγλίας*, μτφ. Μπάρλας Τάκης, εκδόσεις Κουλτούρα, 2016.

Maurois, André, *Ιστορία της Γαλλίας*, μτφ. Πολίτης Κοσμάς, εκδόσεις Όμηρος, χ.χ.

Neveux, Francois, *A Brief History of the Normans - The Conquests that Changed the Face of Europe*, Robinson, 2008.

Nicol, M. Donald, *Βυζάντιο και Βενετία*, μτφ. Μουτσοπούλου Χριστίνα – Αντωνία, εκδόσεις Παπαδήμα, 2010.

Nicol, M. Donald, *Οι Τελευταίοι Αιώνες του Βυζαντίου 1261 – 1453*, μτφ. Κομνηνός Στάθης, εκδόσεις Παπαδήμα, 2012.

Norwich, John Julius, *The Normans in the South 1016 – 1130*, Faber and Faber, 2018.

Oliver, Neil, *The Vikings, a New History*, Pegasus Books, 2013.

Roberts, J. M., *Παγκόσμια Ιστορία* τόμοι Α΄ και Β΄, μτφ. Τριανταφυλλοπούλου Ντίνα - Σταματάκης Νικηφόρος, εκδόσεις Οδυσσέας, 1999.

Runciman, Steven, *Σικελικός Εσπερινός*, μτφ. Αργυροπούλου – Χίλτεμαν Άννυ, εκδόσεις Γκοβόστη, 2003.

Time Life Books, *History of the Gun in 500 photographs*, Time Inc Books, 2016.

Τούντα, Ελένη, *Μεσαιωνικά Κάτοπτρα Εξουσίας, Ιστορικοί και Αφηγήματα στο Νορμανδικό Ιταλικό Νότο*, εκδόσεις Ευρασία, 2012.

Τσιρπανλής, Ν. Ζαχαρίας, *Η Μεσαιωνική Δύση (5ος – 15ος αι.)*, εκδόσεις Βάνιας, 2004.

Zinn, Howard, *Ιστορία του Λαού των Ηνωμένων Πολιτειών - Μια Κοινωνική Ιστορία της Αμερικής από την Εποχή του Κολόμβου ως τις Αρχές του 21ου Αιώνα*, μτφ. Καλύβας Θεόδωρος, εκδόσεις Αιώρα, 2008.

Χαράτσης, Ευάγγελος Έκτωρ, *Το Τάγμα των Τευτόνων Ιπποτών, Η Δράση των Βόρειων Σταυροφόρων στους Άγιους Τόπους και στη Βαλτική Θάλασσα*, εκδόσεις Eurobooks, 2010.

Χαράτσης, Ευάγγελος Έκτωρ, *Εκατονταετής Πόλεμος 1337 – 1453, Η πιο Μακροχρόνια Σύγκρουση στην Παγκόσμια Ιστορία*, εκδόσεις Περισκόπιο, 2008.

Ιστορία του Μεσαιωνικού και του Νεότερου Κόσμου 565 – 1815, Β΄ Γενικού Λυκείου Γενικής Παιδείας, εκδόσεις ΙΤΥΕ Διόφαντος, 2012.

The CIA World Factbook 2020-2021, Skyhorse Publishing, 2020.

www.ingramcontent.com/pod-product-compliance
Ingram Content Group UK Ltd.
Pitfield, Milton Keynes, MK11 3LW, UK
UKHW042011190726
13854UKWH00005B/2244

9 786180 027112